TREATING ADULT SURVIVORS OF CHILDHOOD SEXUAL ABUSE

William C. Nichols, EdD

Consultant
Atlanta and Athens, Georgia

Professional Resource Press
Sarasota, Florida

Published by
Professional Resource Press
(An imprint of the Professional Resource Exchange, Inc.)
Post Office Box 15560
Sarasota, FL 34277-1560

Printed in the United States of America

The copy editor for this book was Patricia Hammond, the managing editor was Debra Fink, the Production Coordinator was Laurie Girsch, and the cover designer was Bill Tabler.

Library of Congress Cataloging-in-Publication Data

Nichols, William C. date.
   Treating adult survivors of childhood sexual abuse / William C. Nichols.
      p.   cm. -- (Practitioner's resource series)
   Includes bibliographical references.
   ISBN 0-943158-68-0 (pbk.)
   1. Adult child sexual abuse victims--Rehabilitation. 2. Incest victims--Rehabilitation. I. Title. II. Series.
   [DNLM: 1. Child Abuse, Sexual--psychology. 2. Child of Impaired Parents--psychology. 3. Incest--psychology. 4. Psychotherapy--methods.   WM 420 N623t]
RC569.5.A28N53   1992
616.85'83--dc20
DNLM/DLC
for Library of Congress   91-50913
                                                                      CIP

<u>DEDICATION</u>

To Sandy and Mike
who don't like abuse and work against it.

PREFACE TO THE SERIES

As a publisher of books, cassettes, and continuing education programs, the Professional Resource Press and Professional Resource Exchange, Inc. strive to provide mental health professionals with highly applied resources that can be used to enhance clinical skills and expand practical knowledge.

All the titles in the *Practitioner's Resource Series* are designed to provide important new information on topics of vital concern to psychologists, clinical social workers, marriage and family therapists, psychiatrists, and other mental health professionals.

Although the focus and content of each book in this series will be quite different, there will be notable similarities:

1. Each title in the series will address a timely topic of critical clinical importance.

2. The target audience for each title will be practicing mental health professionals. Our authors were chosen for their ability to provide concrete "how-to-do-it" guidance to colleagues who are trying to increase their competence in dealing with complex clinical problems.

3. The information provided in these books will represent "state-of-the-art" information and techniques derived from both clinical experience and empirical research. Each of these guide books will include references and resources for those who wish to pursue more advanced study of the discussed topic.

4. The authors will provide numerous case studies, specific recommendations for practice, and the types of "nitty-gritty" details that clinicians need before they can incorporate new concepts and procedures into their practices.

If there are other topics you would like to see addressed in this series, please let me know.

Lawrence G. Ritt, Publisher

ABSTRACT

The need to recognize, assess, and treat a variety of conditions arising from childhood incest or sexual exploitation by kin and other authority figures has recently emerged as a major issue for all kinds of therapists. Many clients have struggled for years without knowing that such experiences were the source of their personal disturbances or without being able to talk about it and find help.

This practically oriented book examines what is known about incest, its multiple causation factors, how it presents (primarily indirectly) in the clinician's office, and its effects on survivors.

Assessment and treatment issues include an emphasis on important signs ("red flags") that alert the clinician to the presence of sexual abuse as an underlying factor in disturbances, on how treating adults differs from treating children, on how one explores and works with survivors - including clarifying communication and comprehensions, dealing with client reactions, normalizing experiences, "going through the valley," reframing, finding trustworthy support sources, jettisoning old feelings, and dealing with the client's family of origin.

A strong and unusual feature is guidance on effective involvement of a married client's spouse in treatment.

This guide is written for therapists and counselors in general practice in all kinds of settings.

PREFACE TO THE BOOK

This work arose out of my clinical experiences and my attempts to integrate them with a continuing study of research and clinical literature that would help me learn to recognize more quickly and treat more effectively the effects of childhood sexual abuse by trusted persons on the clients who came to my offices. I had no training in this area during my professional preparation and, indeed, was not adequately sensitized to the prevalence of such maltreatment of children. Unfortunately, I was not alone; neither were most of the other clinicians of the time, many of them being misled by the popular psychotherapy conception that much of what we recognize today as sexual abuse consisted of childhood sexual fantasies. My work with people eventually began to convince me that all too frequently it was the theory that was wrong, not the client.

We have a lot of catching up and correcting to do, both in terms of recognizing and treating the painful and noxious effects of betrayal and exploitation and in terms of changing the inequitable attitudes and social practices that render the younger and the physically weaker, particularly children and females, susceptible to physical, sexual, emotional, and social abuse.

My deepest appreciation and respect go to those clients who struggled valiantly to come to grips with what was bothering them and who had the courage to share their pain, their shame, their anger, and, finally, their growth and triumphs with me. They helped me comprehend as well as a nonvictim can what it was like to live with the outcomes of their exploitation, and they helped me learn how to understand and help others who had undergone abuse.

If this guide provides the kind of specific guidance that is helpful to clinicians, Sandra Halperin, PhD, a colleague and gifted therapist, is largely responsible. She critiqued two versions of the manuscript, offering perceptive comments and insisting that I provide specific guidelines, "red flags," and examples. She has my gratitude.

W. C. N.

Atlanta and Athens, Georgia
March, 1992

TABLE OF CONTENTS

DEDICATION   *iii*

PREFACE TO THE SERIES   *v*

ABSTRACT   *vii*

PREFACE TO THE BOOK   *ix*

INTRODUCTION   1

WHAT IS INCEST?   3

What We Know about Sexual Abuse   4
What Causes Incest?   7
    Family Pathology   7
    Permissive Subculture   8
    Individual Psychopathology   8
    Alcohol and Alcoholism   9
    Multiple Causation   9

PRESENTATIONS OF INCEST
IN THE THERAPIST'S OFFICE   10

Red Flags for the Clinician   14
Effects of Childhood Incest   18
    A Continuum of Current Effects   18
    Some Female-Male Differences   19
    Victimization and Ethical Issues   20

EXPLORING WITH THE SURVIVOR   21

It's Different from Treating Children   21
Working with the Survivor   23
    Listening Carefully and Understandingly   23
    Clarifying the Client's Communications
        and Comprehension   25
    Dealing with the Client's Reactions   28
    Going Through the Valley   31
    Normalizing Experiences as Much as Possible 32
    Reframing   33
    Exploring the Client's Efforts to
        Deal with the Problem 34
    Dealing with Feelings toward Betrayer and
        Failed Protector   36
    Finding Trustworthy and
        Helpful Sources of Support 38
    Helping the Client to Jettison Old Feelings 39
    Helping the Client Fail and Succeed
        Simultaneously   40
Some Other Issues and Nonissues   41

WORKING WITH THE SPOUSE   42

Married Clients and Their Spouses   42
    Disclosure During Individual Session   43
    Disclosure During Joint Session   45

REESTABLISHING FAMILY RELATIONSHIPS   48

Survivors and Their Family of Origin   49
    Ways of Dealing with the Family of Origin   50
    The Apology Issue   50

SUMMARY   51

CONCLUDING THOUGHTS   52

REFERENCES   53

TREATING ADULT SURVIVORS OF CHILDHOOD SEXUAL ABUSE

INTRODUCTION

A therapist does not have to specialize in working with children, protective services, or courts to encounter cases of incest and sexual abuse. If you are a therapist in a general practice, the chances are that a significant minority of the adults with whom you work are "incest" survivors. Perhaps as many as a third of them were sexually exploited and abused by their kin or other trusted authority figures when they were children. The exploitation could have involved a single event or years of abuse. The victim may or may not have talked to someone at the time of the abuse or received any help then or later.

They possibly did not specify that childhood sexual abuse was a problem when they contacted you. Unless you are labeled an expert or specialist in treating victims of such actions, the chances are that they presented with other problems and complaints. Adult victims of childhood abuse often do not know specifically what it is they are seeking. Some who suffer from the aftermath have consulted one or more therapists over the years or have long been on various medications without childhood sexual victimization ever being considered as a source of their problems.

Along the way some victims will have been labeled "borderline personalities," "hysterics," "post-traumatic stress syndrome" victims, "psychosomatic cases," or given some other diagnosis indicating major disturbances in their functioning. Others will manifest less florid characteristics and generally seem to function fairly well except for some nagging disturbances in interpersonal relationships, some depression, some anxiety, or some disruptions in other areas of their living.

All of us have wasted time when we have failed to recognize that childhood sexual abuse might lie behind the symptomatology or discomfort of such persons. Many adult survivors, therefore, share a need for the therapist to consider the possibility that real childhood sexual trauma may be the source of their difficulties, to assess the situation accurately, and to deal with them sensitively.

Much sexual abuse of children still tends to get concealed. Although some instances emerge as public tragedies and a few cases present to professionals as immediate crisis situations, most evidently remain hidden and are revealed only later in the child's adulthood, if ever. Nevertheless, experts note that during the past 20 years, sexual abuse has been the fastest growing of the types of child abuse recorded in the national reporting system of the United States (Finkelhor, 1985). Whether this represents an increase in the incidence of sexual abuse or, what seems more likely, a surfacing of a problem largely concealed in the past, sexual abuse of children is an important clinical as well as social issue.

It is those unreported and underreported victims from the past that we are recognizing and dealing with more and more in today's practices. Not all adults who have been sexually molested need therapeutic help, but many do.

Therapists encounter child sexual abuse and its effects in two major ways. First, some cases are brought to their attention at the time of occurrence or discovery, when the victim is still a child. The abuse may be the reason that professional help was sought. Such cases may be in a crisis state, particularly if physical force has been used in the course of the molestation. Child sexual abuse also may be revealed during the ongoing course of therapy sought for other reasons by a family with minor children. Experience and research indicate that although intervention at the time of the occurrence is increasing, it is still comparatively rare when the total abuse picture is considered. More often, even today, therapists learn about sexual abuse that occurred when an adult client was a child or teenager. My focus in this monograph is on child sexual abuse that emerges as a clinical issue after the child has become an adult.

The goals for this guide are straightforward: (a) to define and describe incestuous behaviors, (b) to profile the characteristics of adults who survive childhood sexual abuse and the general characteristics of their abusers, (c) to discuss common family and situational dynamics, and (d) to explicate important treatment guidelines and treatment issues. I will provide practical guidance and assistance to therapists to help them recognize the presence of incest-related problems and to increase their effectiveness in working with adult victims.

Before looking at how clinicians determine that childhood sexual abuse is a salient issue in the lives of their adult clients, and before we proceed to help clients deal with whatever aftermath is "historically present" and creating problems in their contemporary living, we need to look at what we mean by incest, what we know about it, and what causes it.

WHAT IS INCEST?

Incest is usually defined legally as a sexual relationship between persons who are prohibited by law from marrying one another. Incest statutes in most states not only attempt to prevent marriages between individuals who are closely related but also try to protect children against sexual abuse by their relatives.

As therapists, we need a different definition and understanding of family sexual abuse in order to work effectively with our clients. The concern in this monograph is not with the marriage of persons of specified degrees of kinship, but rather with sexual exploitation of the young by older and more powerful trusted persons, including family members, in-laws, stepkin, and other caretakers and authorities, and the effects of this victimization when the child reaches adulthood.

For our purposes, incest is defined operationally as the abuse of a child by a parent (or other parental/authority figure) or by a more powerful sibling or other relative for that person's sexual gratification. This definition is intended to cover stepparents and other live-in companions as well as parents who may not reside with the child (a common occurrence in today's single-parent household). Others such as a boyfriend of the mother or teachers are included if they occupy a functional authority/parental role involving trust. This working definition covers any exploitative sexual contact or attempted contact and is not limited to intercourse.

Incest is an abuse of power and a betrayal of trust. Although the actions are sexual in nature, I do not regard them as being as much about sex - although perpetrators engage in sexual acts for

3

their gratification - as they are about abusing power and betraying trust.

Exploitation of the younger and weaker is a major emphasis in my operational definition. Where there is a significant age difference (5 years or more) between the participants, the experience is exploitative of the younger. Some incestuous behavior may be mutually consensual, as in the case of some brother-sister sexual experimentation, and still be abusive. For example, the brother may be physically stronger and the sister may be so intimidated by his greater physical strength or by his favored position in the family that no overt coercion is necessary.

My definition and approach assume that the minor child who is engaged with another person who is older or more powerful is always a victim. In my opinion, it is a disservice to the victim and a distortion of the realities of human development to attribute to children sexual desires and a level of understanding and power that would make them an instigator or consensual peer in such sexual activity. A child's dependent needs for nurturance, touch, caring, caressing, and the like are not the same as adult sexual desires. I am also operating on the assumption that sexual exploitation of a child generally, but not always, is harmful and leaves residuals that affect adult life and adjustment, unless appropriate help and support are provided for the child.

WHAT WE KNOW ABOUT SEXUAL ABUSE

A large amount of adult-child sexual activity was reported in the United States nearly 40 years ago, but the researchers downplayed its negative aspects, and the general public continued to be largely unaware of the magnitude of the problem (Kinsey et al., 1953).

Recent awareness of the prevalence and negative effects of child sexual abuse arose from two sources: the women's movement and the activities of child protection advocates. Feminists concerned with the maltreatment of females established rape crisis centers and shelters for battered women. Discovering that unanticipated numbers of young children had also been sexually abused by relatives, they provided a major push toward securing help for incest victims.

Child protection advocates have focused more precisely on sexual abuse of children by parents and other caretakers and have tended to blame incest primarily on family pathology (Finkelhor,

1984). This attitude implies that family members always contribute to the family pathology that fosters incestuous behavior, a point to which we shall return.

How often does incest occur? The most direct and simple answer is, "*We don't know.*" Solid empirical evidence on the incidence of incest is scant. Some of the best research available indicates that a fourth to a third of adult females and 1 in 10 men were sexually victimized to some extent during childhood (Briere, 1989). The incidence may actually be higher.

Empirical and clinical research provide the following solid impressions regarding incest:

- Males sexually abuse children more than females. This contrasts with physical abuse, where men and women are involved in mistreating children approximately evenly. Most abusive males were abused themselves (Silver, Dublin, & Lorrie, 1969).
- Females are sexually victimized more than males (Adams-Tucker & Adams, 1984; Russell, 1986).
- Children are sexually abused by familiar and related persons more than by strangers. An even greater proportion of the physical abuse to which children are subjected is done by parents. Some research shows stepfathers sexually abusing female children far more frequently than biological fathers (Russell, 1986). But sibling sexual involvement evidently is the most common form of sexual abuse (Banks & Kahn, 1982; Russell, 1986).
- Sexual exploitation does not invariably occur in the context of physical abuse of the victim or other family members. In fact, according to the best research available (Blume, 1990; Finkelhor, 1985), most sexual abuse appears to occur without physical abuse. The dependent position and lack of maturity of children generally make the use of force unnecessary to secure their participation.
- Sexual abuse is perpetrated on children of all ages, from infancy to adulthood.
- Incest is not easily detected when it occurs. The child victim may or may not immediately manifest symptoms that clearly indicate that molestation occurred. Some victims exhibit multiple symptoms, while others manifest no immediate symptoms (Haggard & Reppucci, 1988).
- Incest is not restricted to lower socioeconomic populations. Researchers have found incest occurring through-

out the social structure (Adams-Tucker & Adams, 1984; Russell, 1986).

- The evidence of sexual abuse, as well as physical abuse, appears to be higher in families that are socially isolated, whether the family resides in a rural or urban area (Gelles, 1985). Such families exhibit a blurring of the boundaries between generations and sometimes an extensive breakdown of the family hierarchy, as well as the tendency to isolate themselves from external influences.

Given the fact that males are the major abusers, it seems useful to examine some of the characteristics of men who sexually abuse their children and the characteristics of their families. There is no "profile" that fits all abusers. Clinicians have turned up a variety of personality types who abuse their children. However, we can find clues to some general characteristics of incestuous parents and families (Crewdson, 1988).

Let us look at two men who never met and at their families. Smith, a surly, withdrawn, highly religious, teetotaling, blue-collar worker, built a high fence around his house and lives in the rural south. Brown, a gregarious, party-loving, alcoholic physician, lives in an upper-middle-class midwestern suburban area. Smith kept his daughter out of school after age 14. Brown's daughters attended a prestigious private school as day students. Smith's family rarely left home. Brown traveled with his family on vacations in an expensive recreational vehicle.

Despite their differences, these two men have one thing in common: Both were incestuous parents. Smith impregnated his daughter and reared the child. Brown's incestuous behavior, often conducted under the guise of "physical examinations," was extensive but stopped short of intercourse. They also had in common the facts that both had been sexually exploited as children and both dominated their own families. Smith ruled with physical violence, Brown through the power of his affluence and prestige as a physician. Both men married women who looked up to them, and both assumed that they were entitled to do what they did with their children, rationalizing their behaviors under the rubric of "head of the household" privileges and responsibilities.

Smith's actions were acknowledged many years later when his daughter revealed the parentage to the child of their incestuous relationship. Brown's behaviors came to light when his daughters told their mother what was happening. Their mother had the strength to seek help and to halt what was occurring by removing the children from the situation and divorcing Brown.

Why do people behave as Smith and Brown did?

WHAT CAUSES INCEST?

There is no simple answer to the question of causation. Both professionals and laypersons have advanced a variety of causative suggestions, including family pathology, social isolation, permissive subcultures, individual psychopathology, alcoholism, and others. An examination of some of these explanations is in order.

Family Pathology. Family pathology explanations are often linked with social isolation theories (e.g., such pathological families are characterized by such deep feelings of emotional deprivation and fears of separation and abandonment that the possibility of separation cannot be tolerated; incest - which keeps everything within the family's boundaries - becomes preferable to adultery or divorce as a way of coping with the parents' emotional and sexual estrangements and disappointments) (Sgroi, 1982). As noted previously, family pathology explanations imply that all family members contribute to the family pathology that fosters incestuous behaviors.

Two caveats are in order: First, the assumption that all family members contribute to the incestuous behavior frequently does not stand up under scrutiny. In my opinion, a bedridden and dying mother whose daughter was sexually exploited by her husband, the girl's stepfather, did not contribute to the incestuous incidents - unless one holds her responsible for marrying the wrong man or being too weak to walk or function effectively for several months before she succumbed to a fatal illness. Similarly, a country woman with less than a third-grade education, no transportation, virtually no contact with the outside world, and an abject fear of her brutal husband who threatened to kill her if she defied him, could only be regarded as a victim herself, and could hardly be considered a contributor to his exploitation of the entire family. These are extreme instances, chosen not to prove the point but to illustrate instances in which one of the adults in a nuclear family could not appropriately be assigned responsibility for sexual abuse occurring against children within the family.

Family pathology is a partial explanation in some cases, but certainly not in all instances. One flaw in the simple attribution of sexual abuse to family pathology is that the pathology may just as readily result from the family's reactions to the problematic behavior of one of its members as it may cause the behavior. In some instances, it seems more likely that the pathology is a reaction and result rather than a causal agent.

Although some families in which abuse occurs share certain characteristics, this does not necessarily mean that the families "cause" the abuse or that all members are responsible for its occurrence. Although a family systems perspective is valuable, I am not willing to twist and torture the circumstances that I observe to make them fit a Procrustean theoretical bed.

Permissive Subculture. What can be loosely referred to as a "permissive subculture" explanation also has been advocated (Lubianowicz, 1972; Weinberg, 1976). This is the view that the incestuous behaviors reflect socially acceptable actions in certain subcultures. Examples include the so-called "hillbilly jokes" describing incest as occurring regularly between father-daughter and brother-sister in rural societies; these jokes denigrate females by viewing women as the sexual property of the males. Males in this explanation presumably are not doing anything morally wrong or "crazy" because they are functioning within subcultures whose values tolerate incest.

Even if generally reflective of the subcultures to which such norms are attributed, such an explanation would pertain only to parts of such social groups and would not provide a general explanation for incest. There may be validity to a broader "permissive" cultural explanation in that socialization of males in western society with its emphasis on being sexually aggressive clearly appears to give impetus to victimizing females and children (Finkelhor, 1985).

Individual Psychopathology. Sexually abusive behavior is sometimes ascribed to the individual psychopathology of the perpetrator (Forward & Buck, 1979). When viewing the actions of physically abusive parents or sexual abusers, some people assume that "anybody has to be crazy to do that." This explanation is sometimes accompanied by the idea that perpetrators need therapy, that they can be "cured," that their families can be reunited, and that healthy family life can be reestablished. This view presupposes that the behaviors were something outside the individual's control or that the perpetrator feels conflict and remorse when the actions are acknowledged.

Although the implications of a "cure" orientation are most relevant to the treatment of incest involving minors and their families, they do have some bearing on working with adult survivors. Reconciliation with the exploiter is not necessarily possible or desirable with either child victims or adult survivors. Clinical observation certainly indicates to me that the odds typically are not strong for the genuine "recovery" of perpetrators or the establishment of mature relationships.

Although there may be occasional cases in which a perpetrator is psychotic, this does not generally appear to be a factor. Behaving badly is not the same as being crazy, just as doing something to another person for one's own gratification is not necessarily done because of "craziness" that frees one of responsibility. An individual psychopathology explanation is obliquely useful in that it emphasizes the responsibility of the perpetrator for exploiting the young. A selective process does occur in sexual exploitation. Whatever the predisposing background factors, the vast majority of sexual abuse involves persons who are younger and weaker than the perpetrator. To paraphrase a family violence authority, people sexually abuse others because they can (Gelles, 1985).

Alcohol and Alcoholism. Both empirical research and clinical observations support the idea that alcohol is frequently a factor in abusive behavior, including incestuous actions (Porter, 1984). The most accurate conclusion appears to be that alcohol alone does not cause incest, although it may contribute by dissolving inhibitions against such behavior. The same holds for drugs of various types.

Multiple Causation. Rather than attributing incest to a single cause, the most appropriate explanation seems to be that it stems from multiple causes involving the individual, the family, and the family social setting or context. The most comprehensive multiple factor theoretical explanation, particularly with respect to male perpetrators, has been provided by sexual abuse authority David Finkelhor (1984). He describes a model embodying four preconditions to incestuous behavior that combine psychological and sociological explanations. The model gives attention to psychopathology, socialization patterns, and cultural transmission of values that either prevent or perhaps encourage a predisposition to incest. Finkelhor's work needs to be studied carefully by those seeking a sound theoretical explanation of the causal factors in incest.

Because no single factor adequately explains why incest occurs, multiple factors have to be considered. To borrow a metaphor from physics, incest is a strong possibility whenever a "critical mass" results from the confluence and commingling of a sufficient set of predisposing factors with adequate opportunity. Unlike atomic physics, however, we are not looking at a specific set of factors that will set off the action; rather, there are several possible combinations that can result in a motivational drive that overcomes inhibitions and results in incest.

How does childhood incest present itself to the therapist in adult victims? What effects does such experience have on its victims? I shall not attempt to depict the total impact of childhood incest on adults in detail. Rather, in the next section, I shall describe what is commonly presented in clinical situations, how it is presented, what it means, and how the therapist can respond sensitively and effectively.

PRESENTATIONS OF INCEST
IN THE THERAPIST'S OFFICE

Adult survivors of incest do not present themselves by stating *"I need some help because I was sexually abused as a child."*

In my three decades as a therapist, I do not recall a single adult who has presented childhood incest as his or her initial complaint or problem. That does not mean that I do not have clients who were abused as children, rather, it means that clients typically do not identify childhood sexual abuse as the reason they are seeking therapy.

The presentation picture may change as a result of the increased attention given to all forms of abuse in the last quarter of the 20th century. There is much greater recognition of the existence of incest. In particular, the attention accorded child sexual abuse since passage of the 1974 Child Abuse and Prevention Act has resulted in adults becoming more aware of the potential negative residual effects of childhood incest experiences. In the future, more clients can be expected to gain such awareness and to decide they want professional assistance to help them deal with their unresolved feelings about their exploitation. Still others may recognize that some of their vague psychological problems and confusions may be related to childhood abuse.

Currently, the picture tends to be like this: Incest-related problems are common in adult clients, but we have to be alert to their potential presence in order to make them a part of therapy. Incest as an etiological factor in the contemporary problems of clients is frequently not readily apparent at the onset of treatment.

For example, a colleague in general practice recently estimated that childhood/adolescent incest was a major problem for one-third of the women in her therapy caseload. Most of these women were originally referred by physicians for a variety of emotional problems or because of their continual requests for medication. When their physicians recognized that medication was being sought to obtain symptomatic relief for nonphysical problems, the women were referred for psychotherapy. Incest as a major therapy problem emerged for some of those persons only after the therapist was able to assess accurately the meaning of some of the presenting symptomatology and to probe appropriately into the clients' feelings and history.

The majority of instances of incest that I have encountered in my clinical practice have emerged during the course of marital therapy. That may well be an artifact of my practice, which has always contained a significant number of marital cases. In recent years, marital therapy has comprised the majority of my practice. Regardless, incest that occurred during the childhood and developing years of adult clients typically seems to emerge in therapy (individual or marital) as an afterthought, rather than as the primary or overt reason the person sought therapy. Why this is the case is a complex issue, the answer to which depends on the peculiarities of each individual case.

There is a continuum ranging from clients who can clearly recall and readily discuss the incest experiences to those who have no conscious memory of what happened to them. Major patterns among adult survivors who do not seek therapy to deal with their childhood molestation include persons who:

- Remember but do not regard the incestuous experiences as a problem. Clients may enter therapy with a definite memory of the exploitation but with the idea that "*It was something that happened when I was a child, and it doesn't have anything to do with my anxiety/depression/sexual/marital problems.*" Reactions to incest may be similar to what has been observed clinically with other kinds of sexual exploitation. For example, some adults relate how they regarded an exhibitionist whom they witnessed when they were a child as "odd" and the experience as "funny, and kind of uncomfortable, but no big deal," whereas others continue to be troubled by such encounters.

- Remember but do not mention the experiences. Anxiety regarding incest may be intense among clients who remember but cannot bring themselves to acknowledge or talk about their incestuous experiences. Sometimes, it appears clear that the revelation of incest can be permitted to emerge only after a client becomes sufficiently secure in the therapeutic situation to risk making the disclosure. Even with the most sensitive therapist, some clients can struggle for months (or years) before they are able to bring themselves to talk about their experiences and expose themselves to their stored-up pain and apprehensions.
- Do not remember. Still other clients do not remember the abusive experiences. Their amnesia may be restricted to only the sexual exploitation that they experienced, or it may include lack of recall for all events during a period of time in their lives. Hence, such clients do not seek treatment explicitly for the incest and have no expectations of dealing with that area of trauma during the course of their therapy.

The therapist has to work to effect the needed disclosure in all of these instances, but with the client in control as the pilot. The length of time that it takes for clients to get to the point of disclosing their experience varies greatly among different individuals. Memory may emerge in bits and pieces, and the client may have to take a break and rest afterward. This allows the client time to absorb the effects and become ready to go forward with exploring and dealing further with the childhood experiences and their aftermath. As a colleague noted, *"We cannot tolerate unremitting intensity and pain. By and large, we as therapists can trust that people will remember when they can tolerate it."*

Typically, disclosure emerges when defenses are breached. Examples include:

- "Fatigue" or stress overload. Sometimes the defenses break down because the client is no longer able to devote the necessary psychic energy required to keep the secret out of awareness. The onset of other emotional or practical problems may create an overload that causes the client to seek relief.

- New life experiences. These can bring associations to the client that renew the emotional threats of the earlier sexual exploitation and cause enough anxiety and fright to permit awareness and disclosure. Entering into a marriage, for example, can become the occasion for a loosening of defenses. Also, an experience such as the death of a parent can free the client of formerly pressing reasons for remaining silent and permit disclosure of childhood incest experience.
- Anniversary reactions. Long suppressed or repressed experiences and their attendant feelings and reactions are sometimes brought into the open by developments that provide reminders for the client of the earlier abusive experience. When we suspect that an anniversary reaction is occurring, we can pose questions that facilitate bringing the background issues into the therapeutic arena. For example, we may explore depression or anxiety that cannot be related to current events by asking standard questions such as, "*What kinds of things have happened to you around this time of year in the past?*" This line of questioning often results in the recall and disclosure of feelings relating to anniversary events. A variant of this approach consists of asking, "*What happened to you when you were approximately the same age as your child?*"

Where does disclosure of incest emerge in clinical work if it is not a primary or subsidiary initial complaint? It tends to come forth at two major points:

1. Early in treatment during the taking of a sexual/developmental history or in the appearance of symptomatology that may have an etiological base in abusive treatment. The clinician not only looks for symptomatology that might point to a sexual abuse/incest etiology - such as anxiety, guilt feelings, relationship difficulties, shame feelings, sexual inhibition, sexual activity without emotional involvement, and trust problems - but also asks directly about various kinds of sexual experiences, including abuse and incest. Note that such symptomatology also might point to other etiological factors, and good use

of the clinician's skills in differential diagnosis are needed to ascertain the client's major problems.

At the outset, the client may deny incest experiences, whether the information is sought through a written questionnaire/inventory or through direct questioning by the clinician in a sexual history exploration. When he or she is ready, the same person may later volunteer that, "Yes, there was" sexual exploitation or abuse involving a relative or other trusted authority person.

2. Subsequently during the course of therapy. The clinician picks up clues through reports of symptoms suggestive of sexual abuse and probes again for incest. I pay particular attention, for example, to sleep disturbances and frightening dreams, asking about some of the things that clients typically think about when they are unable to sleep or some of the things that may have disturbed them in their dreams. Some images (such as someone breaking into their bedroom or "bizarre" sexual dreams) have particular salience for the location of incest concerns.

Sometimes, the client has disclosed the incest secret to the spouse and the pair have conspired to continue keeping the secret together. On occasion, the spouse may want the victim to disclose the secret to the therapist but does not feel at liberty to make the disclosure personally for fear of violating the couple's agreement. Experienced marital and family therapists generally can sense that there are discrepancies in what the spouses are relating. The task then becomes one of ascertaining why something is being withheld and of working to gain the trust of the clients so that a more appropriate therapeutic relationship can be achieved and pertinent disclosures can be made.

RED FLAGS FOR THE CLINICIAN

There are certain symptoms that I routinely explore for possible sexual abuse etiology. As noted before, these symptoms and reactions do not invariably point to sexual abuse, but they do so often enough to make such exploration necessary. They include the following:

- *Depression.* Both clinical observation and empirical research (Briere, 1989; Browne & Finkelhor, 1986) support the idea that depression is probably the symptom reported most often among adult survivors of childhood sexual abuse. Once again, other sources may account for the depression, but it could be a sign pointing to a history of childhood abuse, particularly when the depression appears in combination with some of the other symptoms listed below.

- *Anxiety.* The presence of significant anxiety and chronic perceptions of danger all around in the environment should be explored, especially in the absence of situational factors explaining the current anxiety and perceptions of danger.
- *"Self-Defeating" Behaviors.* Among the symptoms that I include under this loose general rubric are suicidal threats or attempts, self-mutilation, repeatedly being a victim of either sexual or physical abuse such as battering (particularly in the case of females), sexual maltreatment and victimization of others (particularly in the case of males), compulsive sexual behaviors, and manifestations of self-hatred such as expressions of feelings of being bad, evil, or shameful.
- *Disturbances in Intimate Relationships.* These include significant difficulties in relating sexually or emotionally (romantically) with another person. For example, some clients may be married and try very hard to relate to their spouses but find themselves unable to "let go" sexually or respond positively even in a more general physical sense when they are hugged, fondled, or intimately touched. In extreme cases these reactions may include total withdrawal from intimate relationships.
- *Borderline Personality Disorder.* The American Psychiatric Association's *Diagnostic and Statistical Manual of Mental Disorders* (American Psychiatric Association, 1987) describes eight assessment criteria for this condition, any five of which are regarded as essential for the diagnosis. As adapted here, they are:

1. Interpersonal relationship disturbances: A pattern of unstable and intense relationships marked by alternation between extreme overidealization and devaluation of the partner.
2. Self-damaging impulsivity: Potentially self-damaging impulsivity in at least two areas such as binge eating,

overspending, reckless driving, sex, shoplifting, or substance abuse.

3. Affective instability: Notable moves from baseline mood to relatively brief moods of anxiety, depression, or irritability that last from a few hours to a few days.

4. Anger: Lack of control of anger or inappropriate, intense anger manifested in constant or frequent displays of anger or recurrent physical fights.

5. Self-Harm: Recurrent suicidal threats, gestures, or actions or self-mutilating behaviors.

6. Identity disturbances: Definite, enduring identity disturbances demonstrating uncertainty regarding at least two of the following: self-image, sexual orientation, friendship preferences, value preferences, long-term goals, or career preferences.

7. "Meaninglessness": Chronic feelings of boredom or emptiness.

8. Abandonment: Marked, frantic attempts to avoid real or imagined abandonment.

- *Histrionic Personality Disorder* (APA, 1987). Formerly called hysterical personality, this personality disorder includes collections of behavior that are intensely expressed, overly dramatic, and reactive in nature, as manifested by people who constantly draw attention to themselves, overreact to events, engage in irrational and angry outbursts or tantrums, or express self-dramatization in exaggerated emotions. Disturbances in interpersonal relationships are expressed by at least two of the following: egocentricity, self-indulgence, and lack of consideration for others; vain and demanding behaviors; dependency, helplessness, and constant seeking of reassurance; manifestations of shallowness even in the face of superficial warmth and charm; and a tendency to engage in suicidal threats, gestures, and attempts.

- *Post-Traumatic Stress Disorder* (APA, 1987). The victim consciously or unconsciously relives or reexperiences the trauma in this disorder. The trauma resurfaces or is expressed in nightmares or disturbing dreams; through intrusive and highly upsetting images or thoughts; in reenactments of the traumatic experiences as a victim or as the perpetrator (a kind of "identification with the aggressor" reaction); or through dissociative experiences.

Perhaps the most dramatic manifestation of this disorder is the reexperiencing of the traumatic experiences in flashbacks, dreams, or nightmares. The dreams or nightmares may portray part of the abuse experience or refer to the molestations through symbolic representations accompanied by feelings of fear and helplessness. Other symptoms may range from hyperalertness to withdrawal and detachment from the outside world, as well as a numbing of general responsiveness, impaired memory (including complete gaps for some periods), disturbances in relationships, and feelings of anxiety, depression, guilt, irritability, and shame.

- *Dissociative Experiences.* Although dissociative experiences (e.g., amnesia, depersonalization, feelings of being more than one person) are part of other reactions and syndromes, they deserve special mention on their own. Dissociation seems to be a psychological mechanism that children use fairly often in their attempts to cope with potentially painful and threatening experiences. The ability to block out pain that is commonly manifested in dissociative disorders helps to explain both how the person tried to cope with abuse as a child and how the person may continue to deal with what would otherwise be consciously experienced as exceedingly traumatic and painful.

  Some clinicians and researchers have described severe chronic child abuse, including sexual abuse, as the factor most closely associated with the most severe and complex dissociative disorder, multiple personality disorder (Hartman & Burgess, 1986). By encapsulating the experience (i.e., internally enclosing it to protect themselves from anxiety and pain and thus splitting the experience off from integration with their ongoing psychic and emotional development), some incest victims split the interior of their psychic world to the extent that multiple personalities occur.

Whenever a client manifests a cluster of the reactions described previously, particularly when there are no other current sources of explanation for the behaviors, the chances are relatively good that probing for abusive experiences will result in disclosure of physical and/or sexual abuse.

EFFECTS OF CHILDHOOD INCEST

Incestuous experiences have both immediate and long-term effects on victims. Our focus here is on the long-term effects rather than on what happens to a child at the time of the occurrence, disclosure, and/or intervention. What do we find when an adult discloses a childhood incestuous experience?

A Continuum of Current Effects. My clinical experience supports the idea of a continuum of effects on adult clients who disclose that they were subjected to incestuous experiences as children. Some have extremely strong reactions that continue to plague their lives (e.g., they manifest some of the symptomatology described earlier such as symptoms of post-traumatic stress disorder). On the opposite end of this continuum, some clients appear unaffected by the abusive experiences.

The continuum of effects of childhood incest demonstrated by adult clients includes cases manifesting:

- Severe current effects. Among my clients, the most dramatic post-traumatic stress disorder reactions (i.e., nightmares, repetitive thoughts, "self-destructiveness") were exhibited by a woman whose denial defenses finally broke down some 25 years after she had been forced into intercourse by a stepfather during the terminal illness of her mother. Unable to handle the dual onslaught of a breaking into awareness of her deeply buried reactions to the molestation and abuse and her long-term rage toward her own domineering husband, she disclosed the source of her distress a few sessions into therapy.

- Moderate to severe current effects. Childhood exploitation of the adult clients with whom I have worked more typically resulted in less dramatic but chronic symptoms that include anxiety, depression, low self-esteem, and long-term problems with trust and confusion regarding family roles and boundaries. Some had never told anyone else about their experiences. Others had told a parent or grandparent who had stopped the abuse. Several persons described their reactions when they were children in ways that clinicians might have diagnosed as a brief reactive psychosis, had a clinician been consulted at the time. (Instead, they had been regarded as "just upset" for a day or a few days, and no treatment was sought.) None of these clients had been involved in either individual or family therapy in connection with the abuse at the time of the original experience or disclosure.

- Minor or no current effects. I have seen some other adults who somehow dealt with the effects of incestuous abuse without any outside help and did a good job of absorbing and integrating the experience into a fairly sound adjustment. Despite careful exploration, the difficulties that caused them to seek treatment and the problems they manifested during the course of therapy did not seem to be related to the incest experience.

Between the extremes sketched here, a variety of responses can be expected; however, my clinical experience indicates that the effects are likely to be closer to the end of residual pain and conflict than to a neutral or more positive outcome.

Some Female-Male Differences. Males are the major perpetrators of sexual abuse on both girls and boys (Finkelhor, 1985). Male sexual aggression and the general cultural theme of male dominance (with all the attendant negative consequences) are thus maintained when the sexual exploiter of a child is a male. These facts, coupled with pernicious sexism in the socialization of children, seem to me to contribute significantly to differential clinical impacts of abuse depending upon the victim's gender.

Stereotypically, females do not tend to get in touch easily with feelings of anger over being abused. With some, whose "trained incapacity" and experience in taking an inferior "one-down" role are prominent, it is exceedingly difficult to help them move past pain and hurt to acknowledging their appropriate reactions of outrage and to begin taking steps to cope with the residuals of their abuse. On the other hand, males are far more likely to move quickly to expressions of anger and prematurely to action, while denying their deep feelings of hurt and pain. Both men and women need sensitive help in recognizing the totality of their feelings, dealing with their abusive experience, and taking appropriate actions to help them move toward healthy contemporary functioning.

Confusion and questions about their sexuality have shown up more strongly among the males with whom I have worked than among my female clients. Not infrequently, males who acknowledge that they were sexually abused as children share with abused females the feeling that there was something shameful about what occurred and that they are not worthy or deserving of satisfactory adult sexual relationships. But some males go the additional step of being fearful regarding their gender identity or actually concluding, *"I'm really gay. I'm a homosexual,"* when their stated desire is to be heterosexual and "a regular guy," as some clients have put it.

In my clinical experience, female victims frequently express feelings of being unworthy and guilty, but their psychic pain and suffering has not appeared nearly so often to result in confused sexual identity. This pattern jibes very well with findings from research that a large minority of females report increased negative feelings, attitudes, or beliefs about men in general as a consequence of being molested and that a much lower proportion indicated that their sexual feeling and perception of sexuality were negatively affected (Russell, 1986).

When the abuser is a male, speculation would be that the female victim (having been in an inferior, dominated position) is less likely to be faced with feelings of having acted inappropriately for her gender than would be a male victim (who has been socialized to be dominant and sexually aggressive - and yet has still been dominated by a same-sex perpetrator). This speculation is further supported to the demonstrable extent that abusive males tend to have been exploited themselves and abused females may continue to be victims.

For the occasion when the abuser is a female, I simply do not have enough clinical or empirical data to permit distinctions between the reactions of females and males whose incestuous sexual involvements have been with older females.

Victimization and Ethical Issues. According to David Finkelhor, a leading sexual abuse researcher, victimization results from adult-child incest even in cases in which the client does not think it has occurred (1979). I think there are some ethical issues for therapists to consider in cases in which clients disclose that adult-child incest has taken place but deny any negative results of the incest. Does the therapist take such declarations at face value and not pursue the matter further? This stance would be taken by those who focus their treatment and interventions solely or essentially on the complaints presented by the client. My own level of ethical comfort requires that I do more; at the very least, I will do sufficient probing and exploring with the client to ascertain whether or not there appear to be any negative effects from the experience.

I do not wish to give clients the impression that they do not attach adequate importance to potentially damaging or shameful incidents in their background. Nor do I want them to believe that they will have major problems if they do not deal with these possible events. What I want is simply to make it possible, and perhaps easier, for them to open up these areas in the future, if in my judgment they do need to resolve issues concerning sexual abuse.

EXPLORING WITH THE SURVIVOR

Therapy generally proceeds in terms of stages or phases. With cases where a history of incest has been disclosed, I typically start working with the survivor alone, and then may bring in the spouse for part of the treatment. In some instances (and after preparing the client), I also work with the survivor's family of origin.

The exploratory process described in this section is an integrative, integrating process in which the therapist helps the client break through old layers of "crust" that hide the original trauma or traumata. This process aids clients in accepting previously denied realities, in processing painful feelings, and in integrating the events, reactions, and meanings into their ongoing thinking, feeling, and living.

IT'S DIFFERENT FROM TREATING CHILDREN

The treatment of the entrenched and encrusted effects of childhood sexual exploitation many years later in an adult client is quite different from the treatment of childhood incest at the time of occurrence. Among the more striking dissimilarities are the following:

- No longer in a child's position of extreme dependency and physical vulnerability, the adult survivor has access to both internal and external resources that were not available in his or her childhood.

  This makes possible the client's participation in therapy in ways not possible for a child. Adult survivors can take greater responsibility for their therapy and can work with their therapists as partners in the change process. Perhaps more than with any other form of therapy, therapy with sexual abuse survivors calls for taking the perspective of the client.

Good advice to the therapist is: If your approach to treatment is to always try to fit the client's problems to your therapeutic approach and style, you will not be able to work effectively with survivors. Effective therapy with incest survivors requires working actively with them in tailoring and individualizing their therapy. The nature of their traumatic experiences and the aftermath of those experiences makes it essential that survivors be empowered in therapy and not be placed once again in a subordinate position.

- Unlike therapy with minor children or teenagers, the focus with adults is not on stopping an ongoing process or protecting the victim from possible resumption of interrupted incestuous behavior. Rather, the emphasis tends to be on dealing with the effects of exploitation in the distant past that affect current functioning.

    The therapeutic task with adults calls for dealing with both the original molestation and the behaviors, consequences, and feelings that have developed and remained with the victim. Adult survivors not only undergo the original trauma but also generally are affected by the behaviors that they have devised in an attempt to cope with the continuing effects of their experiences. Additionally, the childhood victim who continues to be a victim as an adult through periodic or ongoing involvement in exploitative relationships undergoes "double victimization."

    In order to make positive changes, clients need understanding and help in sorting out what is occurring presently and disentangling it from the earlier experiences. Clients need assistance in recognizing that their current painful and "self-defeating" patterns do not occur because "that's how I am" or "that's what I'm like," but because of the lack of resolution of their childhood exploitation. In other words, the presenting behaviors represent coping mechanisms developed in attempts - effective or otherwise - to deal with the original unresolved trauma.

- The involvement of legal authorities and various social agencies that often is part of dealing with child sexual abuse is not a factor when treating adult survivors.

With the disclosure of the sexual abuse of a child, law enforcement, legal, social service, or therapeutic interventions typically occur. The adults with whom I have worked generally had none of those forms of intervention when they were children. Very often, nobody knew about the incidents except the victim and perpetrator. In some cases, the exploitation initially occurred when the child was asleep, and the perpetrator did not know whether the child had ever awakened because the child gave no sign of being awakened by the fondling of genitals.

- The question of whether to remove the perpetrator or the victim from the family is also not an issue as it is with minor children and their families. Adult victims typically have been out of their family of origin and on their own for years.

Please note that this discussion does not refer to current abuse situations where an adult victim may, indeed, need to leave home - temporarily or permanently - in order to avoid additional maltreatment.

WORKING WITH THE SURVIVOR

The first stage or set of small overlapping stages of therapy with a survivor involves uncovering, catharsis, exploration, interpretation, and beginning integration, all in a context of strong therapeutic support. We need a history of the client's reactions and responses in order to determine the severity of the exploitation and what has to be corrected. What has to be undone? What kind of corrective informational and corrective emotional experiences does the client need to undergo in order to get back on an appropriate developmental track?

What follows is a description of general principles and processes for working with incest survivors. Part of this discussion is couched in terms of suggestions to the therapist and part consists of explanation and commentary.

Listening Carefully and Understandingly. What has the client done with the experience internally? How has the client handled what occurred and how he or she felt about it? Has the client processed the experiences or is he or she living with a mass of unprocessed conflicts and problems?

Encourage clients to talk about what happened and their feelings and understandings. Listen sensitively and probe as gently as possible, in order to comprehend what occurred and avoid misperceiving, distorting, and misinterpreting. Or, to put it another way, try to get into alignment with the client's perceptions and feelings and try to interpret as accurately as possible what probably did occur. It is certainly true that what occurred may not be as important in the client's reactions as what he or she thinks occurred and thinks it meant.

Careful listening and patient questioning often open the gate to alteration of the client's feelings and reactions - and thus the impact of the old events and processes - in ways that would never be possible so long as the client's approach to dealing with them remains basically a closed system. What the therapist is attempting to do is to turn this essentially closed psychic system of thinking about and dealing with the old events into a more open system. The therapist's input (and eventually communications from other systems) becomes part of the way clients perceive and deal with their pain and trauma.

For the client, this listening and responding process is both a corrective informational and intellectual experience *and* a corrective emotional experience. As simple as it may sound, the infusion of correct information and the accurate adult interpretation (or reinterpretation) of what occurred in childhood is often a therapeutically powerful experience for the adult survivor.

For example, survivors may have long harbored the idea that they should have done "something" to prevent the abuse. As we explore what evidently happened, it is not uncommon for adult clients to realize that there was very little, if anything, they could have done to prevent the exploitation. Similarly, as they discuss the past situation, they sometimes realize that things could not have occurred as they had been remembering them. For instance, they may realize that it would not have mattered if they had yelled for help, because the fact that the abuser was serving as a babysitter meant that nobody else was around!

The two kinds of corrective experience go hand-in-hand. Sometimes the addition of new information leads to changes in emotional reactions. Sometimes changes in emotional reactions - which stem from being able to talk about the concerns and to experience the emotional acceptance of the listener - lead to changes in intellectual comprehension. At all times, a circular process is likely to be occurring in which it is difficult and perhaps impossible to ascertain the order in which change is occurring and the primary movers - if indeed it were possible to have primary movers - of the change.

Clarifying the Client's Communications and Comprehension. Frequently, what erupts from the client - or slowly emerges, a few words at a time - are reactions to the experience. In a context of acceptance, the therapist listens and seeks to ascertain as much as is necessary in order to comprehend what *probably* occurred, the person's feelings about what happened, and his or her interpretation of the meaning of the events and process.

While listening to clients, I find it helpful in my own thinking to use the following constructs in order to make sense out of their experiences and to get into a position to help more effectively:

- *Event/Process.* I try to obtain as clear a picture or understanding as possible of what occurred and of the processes of treatment experienced by the victim.
- *Perception/Memory.* How did the client perceive what occurred and how he or she was treated? What kinds of memories of the events and of the processes of treatment does the client retain?
- *Feelings.* How does the client feel about the event/process? What kinds of feelings does the client have about the perception and memory? Are the feelings appropriate to the event/process as described and as perceived and remembered by the client?
- *Interpretation.* What interpretation does the client place on what occurred, on what the client perceived and remembered, and on the feelings about all of this? Is the interpretation realistic? The therapist can work to bring change by beginning with a reconsideration of any of these factors: event/process, perception/memory, feelings, or interpretation.

Typically, I begin to express support and as much understanding as I am capable of as the client talks. As this process of uncovering and dealing with the trauma proceeds, I begin to ask questions and indicate, as appropriately and accurately as possible, my comprehension of what I have heard.

I regard it as exceedingly important for the survivor to discuss the details of what happened. This is the case not because of a need to determine any "real truth" or "what actually happened."

Rather, clients generally need to expose their reality perceptions to the external reactions and interpretations of their therapist. Talking with a concerned person outside their personal and family circle often is a critical stage for clients who are trying to break out of the binding straitjacket of denial, fear, anxiety, and fragmentation of self that mark many survivors of childhood betrayal and sexual exploitation. Such sharing with therapists permits victims to test their perceptions of reality against the views and understanding of a knowledgeable person who has not been involved in their lives and thus brings a new perspective to the survivors' morass and confusion.

For example, in order to point out to a client that a child is neither capable of nor responsible for making her parents happy, I might say: *"That's an interesting conclusion that your father reached: He felt you owed it to him to make him happy because the sexual relationship in his marriage was unsatisfactory."*

As the therapist provides new information, offers feedback, and encourages a different intellectual perspective for the adult whose perceptions have remained locked at the stage of childhood experience, such a nonjudgmental approach typically is liberating for the client. Moving through the denial of pain or anger and opening up the underlying affect frees "frozen" parts of the client's self.

Removing the lid from encapsulated, dissociated incestuous experiences has to be done in the same careful ways that one assists clients and discusses other anxiety-producing encapsulated feelings and repressed or suppressed memories. Therefore, I carefully begin to ask the client about details of what happened and clarify my comprehension of what the client says: *"You were asleep and woke up feeling his hand in your vaginal area?"* *"You came out of the shower, and he was there in the bathroom and began to fondle you?"* *"You cried when he forced himself on you, and he said it was your fault it hurt because you didn't relax?"* *"You were frightened and scared of what would happen if he told your mother."*

As information emerges and I begin to get a clear picture of what the client remembers, what he or she thinks happened, and what it meant to him or her, I then begin to make some observations, ask some questions that may cast things in a different light, and generally begin to reframe the experience or experiences in a more supportive - and realistic - fashion: *"What do you think you could have done to stop a 25-year-old man from fondling you? You didn't like it, but there wasn't anybody else in the house. I don't know anything that you didn't do that an 11-year-old could have done to stop things from happening as they did."*

"Your uncle was how much older than you were - 14 years? You had always looked up to him. You had been taught to respect authority. Why shouldn't you have trusted him? You had a lot of basic training in trusting your elders. Up to that time, you had no reason not to trust older relatives."

This kind of exploration permits me to gently challenge and begin correcting misperceptions that have resulted in feelings of shame, guilt, self-blame, or responsibility. My responses to the client depend to a significant degree on what I perceive to be the client's strengths and ability to cope, as well as on the details of what has been described about the experiences. For example, clients who are coping marginally in the present need much more support, reinforcement, and general "building up" before exploring past experiences than those who are doing reasonably well in their current daily living.

There may be a few survivors who require such extensive bolstering to maintain adequate day-to-day functioning that they have no emotional resources available to tackle traumatic past events and work through them. Some need their suppressive defenses supported in order to keep the memories from dominating their present awareness. Certainly, indications of strong anxiety, depression, or withdrawal from reality should alert any therapist to the critical necessity for shoring up defenses and for not proceeding - at least at that time - with exploration of past traumatic experiences.

One therapist who has specialized in treating incest survivors for many years indicates that she now helps her clients deal with the consequences of sexual abuse, rather than talking about the details of the exploitative experience (Butler, 1986). If she means that treatment should go beyond dealing with the initial trauma and that working solely or primarily with what happened in the past is not sufficient, I am in agreement. However, limitations that would omit any exploration of earlier events and feelings has not been necessary or particularly desirable with the clients with whom I have worked. They have been able to talk adequately about what happened to them and to use this disclosure process therapeutically.

In my judgment, both emphases - original trauma and subsequent effects - typically need to be addressed. Exploration of both emphases has been helpful, and occasionally necessary, with most of my clients. At least three overlapping elements appear to be associated with dealing with the two emphases:

1. The abatement of tension, the clarification of reality that occurs when a client shares with a trusted person, and the lessening of feelings of shame and secrecy that come from talking about the original experiences make it possible to deal more effectively with the aftermath. Indeed, such sharing sometimes appears to "pull out the underpinning" of the consequences of the abuse.

    Talking about both original trauma and subsequent effects can establish that it "is all right to talk about" what was put into a secret, "don't tell anybody" category in the past. Failure to talk about past sexual exploitation may subtly encourage clients to feel that their experiences and feelings should not be talked about, thus unintentionally reinforcing the old secrecy and the survivor's sense of shame and powerlessness.

2. Clients' specific perceptions of what they are today and why can be changed as a result of alterations in perceptions and interpretations of the past exploitation.

3. Demonstration of a linkage between what clients are experiencing today and what they experienced in the past can help them to make general sense of their lives.

The more accurately and appropriately one can help clients to see that what they were doing - even when they were engaging in "self-defeating behavior" - was attempting to cope in the best way they could with the aftereffects of the abusive experience, the more effectively one can move toward enabling them to become open to changing their feelings about themselves.

How much does a client need to talk about the past exploitation? Enough. Ideally, enough so that it becomes a part of their historic past and not a living part of their present.

I consider that clients have made a significant step forward in this area when they can talk about their past (and present) experiences and difficulties with a reasonable degree of freedom. That is, they can talk, but they do not have particular needs either to avoid the subject area or to talk excessively about it.

Dealing with the Client's Reactions. What are the client's feelings and reactions to the incest experience? What therapists encounter here depends on a number of factors, including:

1. The extent of the sexual exploitation. Research studies indicate that most sexual abuse cases involve a single occurrence (Haggard & Reppucci, 1988). In general, the longer and more extensive the exploitation, the more powerful the negative impact and outcomes.
2. Whether or not threat or force was involved. Again, the more extensive the use of threat or force, the more profound the negative impact and outcome difficulties.
3. Whether the child was able to procure appropriate help or support at the time of abuse. If the child was able to find acceptance and assistance at the time, his or her ability to deal with whatever persisting problems have surfaced in the present will likely be far greater than if no assistance was available or if he or she experienced further betrayal when help was sought.
4. The child's adjustment prior to the experience. The child who was reasonably well-adjusted and functioning adequately prior to the sexual exploitation is likely to have recovered far more adequately than a child who was not progressing well prior to the experience.
5. Subsequent experiences and personal relationships. What were the nature of the survivor's experiences, networks, and support systems in subsequent years? Was there further exploitation or victimization, or did the client experience support and success?
6. The stability and nature of the client's family and social context, and other factors.

In general, have the experiences, relationships, and significant life systems led the client to view the sexual abuse as an aberration in a generally benign and friendly world or as another example of painful life experience in a hostile and nonsupportive environment?

Leading authorities on sexual abuse (Finkelhor & Browne, 1985) have hypothesized that such experiences can be examined in terms of four trauma-producing factors: traumatic sexualization, betrayal, powerlessness, and stigmatization. There is no clinical evidence that all of these factors will be found in every case, but they furnish a good practical guideline for exploring what the client felt or experienced as a result of the incest occurrences.

A client who was sexually molested by an uncle virtually every time he visited her home over a period of years during her childhood was affected by all four factors. She suffered fear and some physical pain when the relative "cornered" her and fondled and stimulated her on a number of occasions. Physically beaten at the whim of her alcoholic father (a lawyer who was "a pillar of the church" and a person of substance and renown in the community), she not only felt, but indeed was, powerless to avoid or change what happened with either her mother's brother or her capricious father.

Treatment by the significant adults in her home life filled her with a pervasive sense of betrayal at their hands. The cap on her trauma, helplessness, and betrayal was the reaction of her mother when she tried to tell her about the exploitation by the uncle: *"What are you saying! You're lying! I've known my brother all my life. He wouldn't do anything he shouldn't!"*

Bewildered by why the uncle sought her out, she was certain that it was because there was something evil about her, that she carried some kind of sign or stigma that people could spot. It was only after she was an adult and disclosed her experiences in a group for adult children of alcoholics that the woman was able to talk with her two siblings and learn that they had undergone similar experiences at the hands of the uncle. This was a case of a pathological family system.

As with all survivors, she will carry the effects of the childhood molestation and multiple abuse throughout her life. As an adult, however, this woman has made significant progress in dealing with the residue of the sexual traumatization, betrayal, and powerlessness, as well as the sense of stigmatization. This has occurred through a blending of fortunate life experiences and professional assistance. Along the way, she has undergone a large amount of individual, marital, and group therapy.

The marriage that she formed was initially well-suited to the developmental needs of both partners. Neither she nor her husband was initially aggressive in any sense, which permitted each of them to develop a reasonable degree of security in the relationship. Over the first few years, they worked hard and seemingly effectively at establishing and maintaining an egalitarian relationship. Eventually, she was the partner who was ready for change, particularly in the affectional-sexual area. At the beginning of the marriage, she reported, *"Sex was not very satisfying and fulfilling, but at least it wasn't painful and scary and wrong!"* She also declared, *"I'm not helpless now."*

Probably the most significant factor in knitting together and integrating different feelings about themselves for both this woman and her husband has been the experience of parenting. Particularly by treating children - at first foster children and later some of their own - the way they wish they had been treated, these persons have made progress toward blurring the impact of her severe childhood trauma.

Going Through the Valley. Emotionally walking with the client through the "valley of depression" and the "slough of despond" is sometimes a crucial accompaniment to obtaining disclosure of the secret of incest and working on its aftereffects with the survivor. Although empathy is easier spelled than defined - and we really never do know whether we feel as another person feels, only how we feel ourselves - it is critical to apprehend as best we can what the client is experiencing in the disclosure and recall.

Especially in relation to those who fear being overwhelmed by their feelings, the therapist needs "to be" on some occasions, rather than "to do." It would be difficult to overemphasize the necessity of a healing "therapeutic presence" at such times. Essentially all we can do as therapists during some situations is to stay physically and emotionally present with clients while they suffer and struggle. For some clients, their encounter with the therapist may be the first time that they can remember having understanding acceptance and support.

Although we cannot truthfully tell another person, "*I know how you feel,*" we can let him or her know that we are aware of his or her pain: "*I can see that you hurt. Help me understand.*"

With males who are expressing only anger and appear to have bypassed their hurt, it may be necessary to go further in order to help them get in touch with parts of themselves that need to be healed: "*I sense that you were also deeply hurt by what happened when you were a child. That's understandable. You're angry now, and you have a right to be angry, but I'm also concerned about your hurt and pain. It doesn't have to stay there and fester. You use a lot of energy in keeping it locked up. There's not a lot I can do about what happened, but I can sit with you and try to understand as you get to it and face it and work it out.*"

Empathic understanding and assistance do not require dissolving boundaries and blending with the client's emotions. Separateness is required, as is a reasonably firm grip on one's own emotional responses to the abuse. A major reaction is often a sense of helplessness that, unchecked, can defeat the therapist and the therapy. In such instances, case consultation with a colleague often proves very helpful to both the therapist and - ultimately - the client.

There are some ways that the client and therapist can establish and maintain boundaries that aid in dealing more readily with painful affective reactions as the client tries to face and work through surfacing memories and feelings. I have long done things such as ask the client to join me in "objectifying" the "hurt and helpless child of the past" that was abused and neglected and that still exists internally for the client. We then can imagine what it was like for the child. We both can express feelings of sympathy and support for the helpless youngster, as well as other appropriate reactions, and consider possibilities for helping and healing. This is similar to a process that has been described in recent years as "externalizing the problem" (White, 1988/1989).

Abuse cases elicit powerful reactions. Whether or not they deal with abuse cases, therapists who have been personally abused certainly owe it to themselves (as well as to their clients) to secure personal treatment. As they perhaps have told their clients, *"You don't have to carry the baggage of past traumatic experiences around with you without any help or change."*

Normalizing Experiences as Much as Possible. Why explore with your clients? Not to search for pathology. Not to seek to fix a defective personality. Rather, the major purpose is to gain an understanding of the events and reactions that need to be cleared out of the way so that the client's normal stream of growth and development can proceed. The therapist should place the events that are disclosed in a context of normal growth and development whenever and wherever possible. Growth potential and coping abilities are the focus in the exploring I do.

There may be occasions in which it is helpful to insert into the process some descriptions of normal interests and the range of activities in which children engage at various ages and stages of their development. The interpretation and educational work on child development should include an examination of dependency as a major factor in the life of a developing child. The child's dependency on adults and even on other children who are older or more aggressive is a salient factor in exploitation. This should be emphasized by the therapist and needs to be understood by the client. In some cases, it appears necessary and helpful to provide corrective educational information concerning children's ignorance and naïveté regarding human behavior and human bodies, including genital functioning.

A variety of teaching examples is available to the therapist regarding the child's vulnerability. I frequently use simple hand gestures, for example, to point out how when a child is 2 or 3 feet tall, the adult or other person who is 4 to 6 feet in height appears to be a giant, formidable to the "little person." Similarly, the individual who is older or more sophisticated or aggressive easily takes the lead in a relationship. Thus it becomes understandable how exploitation of a younger or more dependent individual occurs. I have many nonsexual anecdotes and recollections from my own childhood or adolescence that demonstrate my own ignorance or ineptness at that time. These anecdotes analogically illustrate how one can be dependent and exploited.

Whenever appropriate and possible - and this is more easily mentioned than illustrated - therapists should respond in ways that indicate that they do not find the client's behaviors or feelings odd, bad, or shameful. The therapist conveys that he or she understands that the client feels or thinks the behaviors were odd, bad, or shameful, going beyond the simple reassurance that *"You shouldn't think that way or feel that way."* I take the stance that the shameful part was the exploitation of a child, that if anybody needed to feel ashamed, it was the aggressor, the exploiter, not the victim. We go through this set of issues patiently and repeatedly, as necessary.

Reframing. Some other useful guidelines and suggestions regarding the exploration include:

- Reframe the events and meanings as positively and accurately as possible, being careful not to minimize the actual pain or other feelings experienced by the client-as-child. For example, it may be possible to point out, *"We know that dealing with this has been very painful. How you dealt with the situation at the time was really quite heroic, though, if we recognize that you were a child coping as best she could. You learned some things about protecting yourself against being betrayed and exploited in the future. We certainly could wish that you had been able to learn self-protection in less traumatic ways, but you used what you learned to protect yourself until you got old enough to comprehend and determine for yourself what was appropriate and good for you in what situation. You made a good learning experience out of your mistreatment."*

- Support the "younger" client insofar as it is possible to do so. Express that support in terms of placing responsibility on the adult.
- Define sexual use and involvement of a child by an older or more dominant person, for that person's gratification, as abuse. Clearly define the use of a child or adolescent by a person 5 or more years older for the sexual gratification of the older participant as sexual abuse. We are not talking about relations between consenting adults. The principle in law that a minor is not capable of executing a legal contract certainly has strong implications for situations in which a child is involved in sexual activity with someone several years older; at the very least, the child is not capable of giving informed consent and entering into "a valid contract."

  There may be some issues of equity in an occasional case in which the "abusee" is slightly below the age of majority and is the dominant figure in the two-person sexual relationship, and the older person is held responsible; however, these are legal issues and not therapeutic issues.
- Be firm in defining sexual abuse as the exploitation of a younger person by an older or more dominant person and locate the definition and understanding clearly in the context of a developmental framework. Once again, what one knew and did at age 5 is different from what one would be expected to know and do at age 25.
- Probe carefully to determine whether the "person as child" was hurt and experienced physical pain and fright during the abuse incident (or incidents). On occasion, the fact that pain and fright were not felt and, in some instances, feelings of pleasure were experienced can be the source of additional confusion for the client. Researchers have found such cases to be extremely rare (Russell, 1986). I have not seen a client for whom the outcome was positive, although I consistently deal with the possibility that some of the confusion felt by them as children may have been related to physical sensations that were pleasurable in the midst of an experience that was exploitative and secretive.

Exploring the Client's Efforts to Deal with the Problem. One of the pertinent questions in dealing with all kinds of difficulties in therapy is, "*How have you tried to handle this problem?*" Incestuous experience is no exception. The therapist needs to know and to understand clients' past efforts to deal with their experiences. If clients have not revealed in therapy what they attempted to do at the time or subsequently, I will ask such questions as, "*Were you able to tell anybody about it?*" If so, "*What happened when you tried to tell?*" "*What did you expect to happen when you told them?*"

These questions are asked because it is important to know whether clients did attempt to tell anybody and how they were treated if they did: Were they believed? Were they supported? Were they rejected and made to feel guilty or ashamed? Were they punished otherwise? Some research indicates that approximately a third of those who have been abused have never told anybody (Finkelhor, 1985).

If they tried to tell someone (particularly a significant authority figure) what was happening to them and they were treated poorly, this usually makes it harder to gain their trust in therapy. They have already suffered at least "double betrayal" at the hands of the perpetrator and the failed protector, who did not trust them. As therapists, we have to deal not only with the effects of the abuse trauma but also with the rejection and rupture of trust that resulted from our clients not being believed or supported by the parental figures on whom they were dependent.

Trust has to be built carefully and incrementally with all survivors of incest: those who have told and had a bad result, those who have not told, and those who have told with a good result. If they have not previously told anyone, it may be hard to get them to talk about their experience, although they do not have to struggle through the scar tissue of an intervening negative experience that occurred when they tried to get relief. If they had a supportive experience when they told authorities, that typically provides a base on which to build. Sometimes, it is necessary to point out with considerable sensitivity and care that the help they got at the time was not necessarily flawed because it did not "fix things" for them for all time.

In my judgment, the most important factors in a trust-building process pertain to "believing the client's pain" and being reliable and trustworthy in our dealings with the client. This means that we are aware that what clients are recalling may not be accurate in all details and may be quite distorted in some instances, but, at the same time, we believe that they were hurt and that they have undergone bewildering and painful experiences. Also, it means that we treat them with respect and keep our promises. For example, I think it is exceedingly important to be on time and to help them begin to recognize that the therapist will deal with them in predictable ways and with integrity.

Dealing with Feelings Toward Betrayer and Failed Protector. During exploration, the therapist should look for reactions of the client not only toward the abuse but also toward the perpetrator/abuser and toward the parent/guardian whom the child expected to serve as a protector and who did not do so. To acknowledge what the perpetrator/betrayer did is to acknowledge that the client's world was not as safe and protective as it should have been. Of course, in cases in which one of the parents was the perpetrator and the other the failed protector, both parents may be regarded as betrayers.

Clients generally recognize their feelings toward perpetrators more readily than their reactions toward the failed protector. Anger and other feelings (including contempt and revulsion, which are occasionally still laced with fear) can generally be witnessed toward the perpetrator without difficulty. It is the anger and sense of hurt and betrayal toward the failed protector that are more subtle and difficult to reach, but probably are more crucial in the client's healing and growth process.

It is sometimes readily apparent to the therapist but not to clients that they feel disappointed in or angry toward the parent they looked to for support (e.g., usually the mother). Clients often have difficulty opening up denied feelings toward the failed protector. In some instances, client reactions may be displaced as feelings of anger harbored toward "life in general," toward the circumstances or "fate" that "caused this to happen to me," rather than disappointment or anger with regard to the perpetrator or failed protector.

Several fairly distinct, sometimes overlapping, stages of reaction can be discerned in the client's feelings regarding the perpetrator and the failed protector. Clients need to be helped to move through these stages:

- Initial feelings of hurt, confusion, and bewilderment. These initial feelings tend to persist in the more heavily traumatized survivors whose socialization and life experiences have "trained" them to accept abuse as their lot. For these survivors, the first step forward consists of gaining the strength and self-confidence to experience and acknowledge their feelings toward those who betrayed them. For the survivors who express only anger, there is a need to help them recognize and acknowledge their underlying hurt and pain before they can appropriately move through the stages.

- Feelings of anger. The initial feelings of hurt, confusion, and bewilderment that frequently emerge are typically replaced or at least joined by feelings of anger. I generally regard it as a sign of progress when the client is able to acknowledge feeling pain as well as anger. It is vital, in my judgment, for the therapist to understand the loyalty conflicts - and the resultant fear and guilt - that clients may experience as a result of recognizing and acknowledging that the person who should have protected them abused them or failed to protect them.
- Loss and mourning related to trauma. Grieving over the absence or loss of a safe and supportive environment and protective parents goes on throughout the process of disclosing and working with the feelings and knowledge that emerges in therapy. However, as a comparatively distinct stage, loss and mourning seem to be most clearly found following the major anger phase. Wherever and whenever feelings of sadness and loss become evident, the therapist needs to make time to work them through as completely as possible. New expressions of the mourning process will outcrop later.
- Loss and mourning related to normal growth and development. I refer to this process as "helping the client accept her or his orphanhood." This is a part of normal growth and development (i.e., accepting the fact that parents fall short of our expectations because of their own limitations and the unreality of our expectations in some instances). In order to mature, it is necessary for all of us to recognize the extent to which we cannot rely on our parents.

This should not be misinterpreted by the reader as a façile statement implying that all we have to do is to recognize that we have to stand on our own feet. This is particularly true with regard to our betrayed clients. The betrayal and failed protection experiences of children who have been abused certainly are more serious and difficult to deal with than the more typical and normal shortcomings in the parenting behaviors of most of us.

- Disrespect and contempt. As with other kinds of reworking of feelings toward a parent, the initial feeling of awe or fear with which the (perceived as) omnipotent parent is regarded is generally replaced eventually with feelings of disappointment because this parent did not measure up to the idealized image held by the disillusioned offspring. That is, the revered or feared parent is no longer revered or feared, but is regarded as a failure and sometimes with contempt because of the failure.
- Tolerance and acceptance. I work very hard to help the client get past the contempt - sometimes hatred - stage. As is the case with the client's ability to acknowledge and work with pain and anger and to let the mourning process go forward, manifesting the ability to get past feelings of rejection and contempt because a parent failed represents a positive step in the client's therapy. This does not refer to achieving a new form of denial or sugar coating one's perceptions. Instead, it refers to reaching the point of genuinely accepting the fact that one's parents are whatever they are, for better or worse. Until clients achieve tolerance and acceptance, they are likely to be preoccupied with wishing their parents were something else or continuing to be consumed with hurt and anger.

   This does not imply anything regarding the kind of relationship or lack of relationship that the client maintains with the perpetrator or the failed parent. Rather, in the simplest terms, it refers to gaining a relatively realistic acceptance of what one's parents are like and what can be expected of them.

Finding Trustworthy and Helpful Sources of Support. Working with the anger toward the failed protector may be crucial in helping clients gain a workable degree of trust that will enable them to begin making satisfactory progress in resolving the effects of the old traumata. Frequently, the failed protector is the parent toward whom the client intuitively perceives it is safe to feel anger. Simultaneously, this parent is also frequently the person whom the client perceives as potentially offering support in the present (as in childhood). In some cases, such support may be essential in allowing the client to trust sufficiently to grow beyond the point at which his or her growth was stunted.

   If possible, I want to find someone important in the client's childhood around whom the client can establish feelings of reliance and dependency and thus "backfill" childhood losses and pain to the greatest extent possible. If I can establish with clients that there was somebody in their childhood years who cared for them or at least was benign and that they could trust to treat them well and appropriately, we have taken a step toward creating the perception that they were treated as if they had value, and we thus have some basis for reinforcing their sense of future self-worth. Although not everybody treated them as a person of worth and value, somebody significant did! Hence, the perpetrator was the one who was out of line. With adults, it is occasionally possible for the client to reestablish or strengthen a present relationship with such persons who were helpful in the past and to enlist them as a helpful current source of support.

Helping the Client to Jettison Old Feelings. When the client is still harboring feelings that the experience "ruined my life," the therapist faces the issue of providing appropriate understanding and support while stopping short of encouraging or even indulging the client in perpetuating unproductive reactions. Although I may risk being misunderstood and misinterpreted, I am going to try to illustrate the kind of interventions that I think are helpful, and often necessary, in order to help some clients break their cycles of continuing anger and resentment.

One may respond, at a point in treatment where clinical judgment indicates that some straightforward dealing with the residual resentments is appropriate, somewhat as follows:

Therapist: "Agreed. He *was* a lousy son-of-a-bitch for doing what he did. It wasn't right. You were treated badly. You were mistreated, abused through no fault of your own. You had reason to get angry, but your anger is not doing anything to him. You're the one being hurt by your resentments now."

Client: "But it's ruined my life."

Therapist: "It has had a big impact. No question. And I wish that it hadn't happened. But can you think about not letting it go on ruining your life?"

The purpose here is not to "beat up on" the perpetrator of long ago, but to help the client recognize, deal with, and let go of old nonproductive thoughts and feelings. As implied previously, this kind of intervention and encouragement by the therapist should be restricted until a strong therapeutic relationship exists.

It is also important that what the client is being asked to give up can be (or already has been) replaced by new productive thoughts and feelings.

For example, one occasionally finds intelligent clients who can recognize their anger or other strong feelings but have not yet internalized the idea that they do not have to act on these emotions. A young professional woman with whom I worked several years ago would initially fly into a rage and strike out physically whenever she became angry with her husband. She began to follow my suggestions of getting away from the scene temporarily whenever she began to feel the familiar feelings of rage, leaving the house for a walk around the block or down to the park until she cooled off. After some time, she said, "*You know, I never knew that you could deal with your anger.*" She went on to point out that what she had seen in her family of origin were patterns of either completely denying that one was angry or exploding. In her family, acknowledgements of anger inevitably meant one had no control or recourse except to let the anger out by shouting and other physical expressions. She gave up the physical expression of her anger (toward her husband and objects) when she recognized that she had gained the ability to exert mastery over her behaviors.

Similarly, some clients seemingly do not know that they do not have to continue carrying and stoking their resentments. Eventually, I may say to some of them, "*Give it up. You don't have to keep corroding your insides.*" Once the client has been able to accept appropriate support, the emphasis during this empowerment process is on the power and ability of the client to deal with the residue from the old experiences.

Helping the Client Fail and Succeed Simultaneously. Building on whatever foundations and indications of strength and coping abilities I have found in my clients, I can begin to increase their sense of empowerment. With any new step or behavior, I try to help the client deal with setbacks when he or she tries something and does not completely succeed.

We start this process by trying to help them set realistic expectations when they discuss a contemplated new action. I will point out, for instance, "*You are not going to succeed every time or in every way. Nobody bats 1,000.*" When they make an attempt to achieve something they desire and achieve partial success, I emphasize what they have accomplished, taking a "Pollyanna" or "best light possible" approach. Sometimes, the positive factor that can be recognized and supported is simply the fact that they attempted to take a positive step. Therapists become cheerleaders in such situations.

This process works with clients over and over again. It is a process that requires patient repetition and a genuine commitment on the part of the therapist to making strongly discriminatory judgments and "calling the shots as they are." To offer support lavishly or without some valid basis is to be less than honest with clients and strains one's credibility, to the detriment of the therapy and the client.

SOME OTHER ISSUES AND NONISSUES

There are a few cases in which the client willingly participated in incest as a child. This leaves the question of the client's feelings about his or her participation for us to tackle. If there is no residue affecting their lives, there may be no treatment issue. However, when there are continuing effects that disturb one's life and current adjustment, there are treatment issues to be addressed.

Some sexual experimentation between peers falls into this category. Therapists can always claim that there are treatment issues if one searches hard enough; however, I do not find that peer incest (where there was no significant age difference or threat or force involved) presents the same kind of outcomes clinically as situations involving threat or force between siblings or cases of adult-child involvement. Sometimes, it seems appropriate and accurate to interpret the behaviors in developmental experimental terms. Some exploration with the client often discloses that the children were experimenting as part of their developing sexuality. The experiences of curiosity and stimulation may have been stronger than the barriers and the guidelines for appropriate behavior that they had internalized. Their actions were premature and the partner inappropriate, but this was part of learning. Much of our learning is trial-and-error, and it certainly is accurate to so characterize some childhood sexual experimentation with peers.

Victimization certainly can occur without clients feeling that they have been victims. For example, the client could be robbed of normal developmental opportunities through the actions of an older family member without knowing that such was the case. An outside observation discloses that such loss occurred. In my judgment, the loss is just as real, although somewhat different in outcome, than if the victim knew at the time that he or she had been deprived of normal and typical developmental opportunities. Not infrequently, victims who are not aware they are victims are still in a state of bondage to the definitions of life and role promulgated by the abusing adult family figure. It is only when they have adequate opportunity to compare their experiences with those of others that they begin to suspect or comprehend that they have been deprived and abused. In systems terms, when a rigid system's boundaries are loosened up and become permeable so that more information is available from the outside and a stronger interchange can occur, clients become able to break up their emotional bondage patterns.

WORKING WITH THE SPOUSE

If the victim is married, treatment interventions pertaining to family initially are concerned more with the spouse than with the client's family of origin, because the marriage is the relationship that is most immediately affected. Spousal interventions have the potential for either facilitating treatment or undermining it. The marital relationship itself may be either helped or threatened by what occurs in therapy. Family-of-origin issues, including the questions of confronting the perpetrator and dealing with the family itself, come later in the treatment process.

MARRIED CLIENTS AND THEIR SPOUSES

If the client is married, the family-related issues that the therapist faces at the outset typically are concerned with the knowledge and role of the client's spouse. What does the spouse know? How has the spouse reacted to any knowledge or suspicions about the childhood sexual exploitation of his or her marital partner? Should the spouse be involved in the therapy? If so, at what stage and in what ways? Do we, now or at a future stage in treatment, work on the issues resulting from childhood sexual trauma and the incest healing process with the spouse present? The best answer to these important questions is *"It all depends."* How did the disclosure come to the therapist and what did it reveal about past and present events and feelings?

Disclosure During Individual Session. Did the victim tell the therapist about the childhood exploitation in an individual session, either during an assessment stage at the beginning of treatment or sometime later in therapy? If so, the following points furnish some guidelines for proceeding.

- Did the client indicate that the spouse did not know about the incestuous events? If the spouse does not know, how does the client feel about the spouse knowing (Positively? Neutral? Negatively?)?
- Did the client indicate that the spouse knew and should be present while the client works on any of the issues related from the experience?
- Did the client protest that he or she feared having the spouse know or be present?
- Does it appear desirable and possible to try to ameliorate the fears of the client through exploration and support with the goal of eventually informing the spouse?
  If the spouse presumably does not know about the abuse, what reasons may there be for sharing the secret with him or her?
- Does the client wish to share with his or her spouse for reasons that appear solid and reasonable under examination (e.g., a need to decrease personal feelings of shame, fear, and doubt by socializing the experience through sharing with a trusted partner; a need to provide the partner with a more adequate basis for understanding the client)?
- Are the spouse and the marriage being negatively affected by the unresolved effects of the abuse and the client's current difficulties? Are there indications and beliefs on the part of the client that some immediate relief and help can be brought to the spouse and marriage by sharing information and understandings that have recently emerged for the client?
- Attempts by the client to change as a result of being in therapy will affect the spouse and the marital subsystem of the family and may elicit reactions that hinder further change. A systemic view and my clinical experience indicate that at least the neutralization of potentially oppositional reactions or, hopefully, the enlistment of a spouse in support of a client's treatment is the preferred route whenever possible.

On the other hand, there certainly are times when informing spouses and attempting to enlist their neutrality or support may be contraindicated. These include:

- Any circumstances that would place the client at risk for further sexual, physical, or emotional abuse.
- The absence of indications that the client could assimilate the information effectively or indications that the spouse would be unable or unwilling to respond in a supportive fashion.
- Resistance of the client to informing the spouse that continues after careful and sensitive exploration of the pertinent issues.

A note of caution is due here: If there is any significant question in the therapist's mind about informing and involving the client's spouse, I think it is better to err on the conservative side by delaying disclosure. Timing is everything in clinical work. If the client is not ready or the spouse is not ready, then it is not the time to disclose the abuse to the spouse, regardless of whether he or she "knows at some level." If incest is disclosed prematurely, the damage is done and the disclosure cannot be recalled. It is like exposing a dandelion to the wind and watching the "little parachutes," as children sometimes call them, scatter beyond possible recall. On the other hand, it is always possible to disclose at a later date something that has not been shared.

If the marital partners have known each other for at least a few years and the secret has not been shared, the victim who wishes to make a disclosure to the mate often needs assistance in effecting that communication. My preference is to have the victim inform the spouse, provided he or she is able to do so. This can be done either in a conjoint session or outside the session, if the client prefers to do it that way. We typically take some time preparing the client, going through the client's feelings and apprehensions, and sometimes role-playing how he or she will inform the spouse.

If the spouse is informed in a conjoint session, it may be necessary and helpful in some cases for the therapist to set the stage in the session, informing the spouse that his or her partner has something to share, that it has not been easy for the other person to get to this point, that the issue to be discussed is important to both of them, and that the spouse's support and understanding are needed. Afterwards, any assistance that seems indicated for dealing with the issues raised by the disclosure and reassurances about continuing help can be given.

Does the therapist assume the role of telling the spouse if the victim is not able to do so? This can be done in some cases, however, this is once again a matter of clinical judgment. My criteria are primarily my impressions that the client genuinely wants the spouse informed but needs the support that would come from having the therapist provide the information in a context of nonjudgmental reporting and sharing.

Disclosure During Joint Session. Did the disclosure come during a conjoint session with both the client and spouse present? My experience has been that when disclosure in therapy came during a conjoint session, the spouses had already talked about the childhood exploitation before coming to my office. Frequently, the spouses had urged their mate to bring the issues into therapy because they hoped to try to get some help for their partner and for the marital relationship.

Whether or not the partners have already discussed the presence of childhood exploitation, there is always the question of whether the nonvictim "knows" or strongly suspects that it occurred. In almost all cases with which I have dealt, the spouses already had some idea that something problematic existed with their partners. The spouses typically "knew at some level of awareness" that there was some degree of strain, tension, distance, or awkwardness and frozenness in the relationships between their mates and the mates' parent, sibling, or other relative or childhood authority person.

"*I always knew that there was something wrong, something not right between* _____ *[the spouse] and* _____ *[the perpetrator/betrayer].*" This is a typical statement of spouses following the disclosure. Sometimes, this is accompanied by the assertion, "*I'm glad to get this out in the open. I knew something was there.*"

There is also the possibility that the spouse's motivations are not aimed at getting help in order to produce a better and more satisfactory relationship. Rather, the spouse may wish to get the client into therapy in order to minimize his or her guilt over a previously made personal and secret decision to leave the marriage. That is, if George can get Mary into treatment so that she "is taken care of," it will be possible for him to get a divorce without feeling that he has really abandoned her.

This is not the place to discuss in detail the therapist's responses to having a client "dumped on the office doorstep" by a spouse who contacts a therapist and then leaves the marriage. For the purposes of this monograph, it should be sufficient to note that such rejection and abandonment of the client is another major blow to self-esteem and feelings of self-worth. The client and therapist are faced with a difficult and painful therapeutic experience. Anxiety, depression, anger, and panic are common reactions. Occasionally, serious withdrawal from reality occurs. The therapeutic tasks are similar to those of other severe bereavement and grief situations embodying extreme rejection and abandonment.

When disclosure comes with both spouses present, the following guidelines for deciding what to do and how to proceed can be helpful:

- What are the strengths of the marriage?

     If the marriage is clearly at the point of dissolution and a firm decision has been made by one or both of the mates to end it, I feel that my first responsibility is to the abuse survivor. Secondarily, I feel that it is responsible behavior to help them complete their dissolution process humanely or to help them find someone else to aid them in this process, if they are both amenable to this course of action.

     If the future of the marriage is uncertain, I feel a responsibility to provide assistance to the couple in increasing their ability to communicate and resolve differences effectively so that they can examine more realistically and with greater clarity their degrees of commitment to the marriage and caring for each other. I would suggest that any immediate decisions about the future of the marriage, particularly ending the relationship, be held in abeyance until the immediate issues of dealing with the sexual trauma and its aftermath are adequately resolved. Whether the spouse becomes a resource and is involved in the support and treatment of the survivor depends to a significant degree on the progress made in stabilizing and strengthening the marital relationship.

     If the marriage is currently strong (or if the commitment, caring, communication, and ability to deal with conflict and effect compromise can be made relatively strong), it makes good sense to me to draw on the marriage and plan to involve the spouse in the treatment at appropriate points.

- How well have the couple dealt with the issues, according to the therapist's best assessment and impressions?

  This refers specifically to whether the partners have been reasonably successful in talking about and responding to the challenges to their relationship brought about by the knowledge of the abuse or whether it has driven them apart and threatened their adaptation and coping abilities. If they seem to have fared reasonably well in their efforts, the spouse and the marriage will be regarded as resources. If they have not and the results have been divisive and threatening to them, it certainly will not be possible to rely on the spouse at the outset (and perhaps not at all).

  Another aspect of spousal involvement is the client's and therapist's perception of whether the spouse has been understanding and supportive. If not, what are the possibilities for helping the spouse gain adequate acceptance of his or her mate and to assimilate knowledge of the abuse so that it is not threatening? A few individual sessions with the spouse focusing on education, exploration of ideology, and clarification of feelings can in some instances accomplish a great deal. If the spouse is not available for such exploration or continues to exhibit negative reactions, the therapeutic process focuses on the survivor, with careful monitoring of the reactions of the uninvolved spouse.

- What is the spouse's relationship with the victim's family?

  Is there sufficient objectivity in the spouse's feelings about and relationship with the client's family to permit him or her to deal with the knowledge of the childhood exploitation without making things worse for the client? For example, if the relationship between the spouse and the client's family is so fraught with anger, dislike, or general negativism that the reactions of the spouse take precedence over the needs of the survivor, not only can the spouse not be relied on for assistance but also considerable effort from the therapist may be required in order to avoid harm to the client.

- What do the client and the partner think should be done?

  This question needs to be explored with particular care. Do both partners wish to work on the reactions to the sexual exploitation as part of marital therapy, at a stage agreed upon with the therapist? If so, and the other criteria listed support this approach, I typically start moving treatment in that direction. If one or both of them have reservations about such an approach - and the reservations continue after exploration of what is involved in their reluctance - I consider the timing not appropriate for marital therapy. I also consider the possibility that I have missed something and may do some probing into areas that my knowledge of the couple indicates might be involved in their reluctance to conjoint therapy.

- What is the clinician's assessment of the pros and cons of involving the spouse as a supportive force and perhaps even as a kind of cooperative helper in the client's treatment?

We have been dealing with this criterion at least implicitly and at times explicitly throughout this discussion. If the spouse is present and involved in the survivor's therapy, I find myself continually trying to monitor the questions:

- Is the spouse sufficiently understanding and supportive to be helpful in the treatment of the survivor?

  I have often found a wife or husband capable of shedding valuable light on their spouse's family-of-origin relationships and problems. Through their insight and support, they sometimes can render unique assistance in effecting change in conjoint treatment in a variety of areas (including reactions to sexual abuse in some instances). Sometimes, a spouse may not contribute actively to the survivor's progress but may provide a kind of passive support and also can be deterred from becoming threatened by being left on the outside of therapy wondering what is happening and perhaps feeling rejected.

- Is the spouse becoming threatened and reacting in ways that may undermine the client's progress?

  If so, a change in the treatment plan is indicated. The spouse may need to be seen individually for a time or, in rare cases, referred to another therapist.

REESTABLISHING FAMILY RELATIONSHIPS

Family reconstruction (so that the members can live together) is not necessarily a goal in the treatment of adult victims of childhood incest as it typically is in the treatment of children or adolescents and their families. There are no questions regarding removing anyone from the family home or whether the perpetrator or the victim should be removed. The victim has already left the family for an adult life. With an adult survivor, one does not have to be concerned with such issues as resolving a crisis about facing the community, as is the case when the victim is a child or adolescent who goes back to school immediately after the abuse has occurred.

SURVIVORS AND THEIR FAMILY OF ORIGIN

There are some current life issues that are important in the treatment of abuse survivors. For example: *"What is the current adult relationship between the client and the perpetrator of the exploitative action?"* *"What is the relationship between the client and his or her family of origin?"* *"How has the client attempted to deal with the perpetrator and the family of origin?"*

Ideally, one hopes to be able to help clients rework and reestablish relationships in their family of origin (where the incest occurred). This is not to imply an idealized view of family life in which it is essential to "make everything all right" between the client and the family of origin. Rather, to the extent that the occurrence and its sequelae have dammed up the normal development of family-of-origin relationships, the general goal is to clean out the interferences so that such development for the client can proceed at an adequate and appropriate pace and, if possible and desirable, so that more comfortable and easy relationships can be established with members of the family of origin.

In some cases, it is not possible to resolve problems with the family of origin. Key players may be dead or mentally disabled to the extent that working out old issues and bridging across them cannot be accomplished. Similarly, there are cases in which important signs indicate that any attempt to resolve problems would be so strongly resisted or there would be such negative reactions toward the client that it is not desirable to try to work with family-of-origin members. For example, obvious contraindications for working directly with the family of origin (or encouraging the client to do so) would be indicators that physical violence could result or that renewed or continued emotional abuse would result.

Ways of Dealing with the Family of Origin. As with other issues involving a client's family of origin, there are essentially three ways of helping him or her deal with them. Beginning with the most direct, the therapist prepares for and conducts family-of-origin sessions in which the client and therapist meet with the members of the client's family in one or more sessions. This intervention has been described at various places in the family therapy literature, including my own writings (Framo, 1982; Nichols, 1988).

A second intervention involves coaching the client on how to "go home again" and deal with family members about unresolved issues from the past. This also has been described in the family therapy literature (Bowen, 1978; Nichols, 1988).

The third procedure is one in which the client is assisted in dealing with his or her reactions and in establishing ways of functioning that do not involve attempting to deal with family-of-origin members. There may be some instances in which the client's decision to cut loose from the family of origin makes good sense and warrants the therapist's support and reinforcement. Spouse confirmation of the situation involving the client's family of origin is particularly important in cases where there is some question as to the advisability of attempting to effect changes with the family.

The Apology Issue. Some of the approaches to dealing with incest call for having the perpetrator apologize to the victim in a session in which the entire family is present ("Madanes Presents," 1989; Trepper & Barrett, 1989). The apology issue is quite different with an adult victim of childhood incest than it is with a child victim where intervention occurs in close proximity to the incidents of abuse. Unlike children, the adult victim typically is no longer in a position of economic and physical dependence on the perpetrator. As adults, clients are generally capable of making decisions without depending on the perpetrator. Equally important is the fact that an adult has the knowledge and the capacity to comprehend and interpret experience that is lacking in children.

The therapist is not in a position to require the perpetrator to apologize, even if the therapist thinks such an act would be helpful to the victim. No legal force or court authority backs the therapist and client. The abuse occurred many years earlier. Often the perpetrator is not even readily accessible. In some instances, the perpetrator is dead.

The important thing in most cases with which I have dealt has not been that the client receive an apology from the perpetrator in front of the victim's assembled family of origin. The client is no longer living in the family of origin and does not need the assurances of protection for living in that group that apology sessions imply. Rather, the important thing seems to be an acknowledgment by significant persons that the client was wronged and that he or she is all right as a human being.

If possible, acknowledgements that the client has been wronged are very helpful; however, these acknowledgements can come from significant persons other than the perpetrator. Given the fact that the victim is now an adult and not subject to the authority and control of the abuser or failed protector, it is much less necessary to hold an apology session to make the environment psychologically safer for the survivor.

In my opinion, the most important issue generally is the ability of the client to recognize that he or she has a network of support available and that significant persons recognize that exploitation occurred and are accepting and committed to supporting the client in the present and future.

SUMMARY

In this practically oriented guide, I have attempted to approach the important set of issues arising from the long-term effects of childhood sexual abuse as they are encountered by therapists. If I have been successful in sensitizing clinicians to the prevalence of histories of childhood sexual abuse and to the need to understand this phenomenon and its effects on those adult survivors, I will have met my first objective. If I have succeeded in providing clinicians with some useful guidelines for dealing with survivors within the framework of their ongoing treatment philosophy and methodology, I will have met a second objective. If I have opened the doors to some new procedures that clinicians can use to aid in the healing of the childhood traumas that are often so painfully "historically present" in exploited and abused clients, I will have met still another objective.

I have not attempted to discuss all the ways that interventions can be made and assistance provided to adult survivors. Group therapy, art therapy, and self-help and support groups all are used in dealing with the difficulties of survivors. All have contributions to make. However, the focus here has been on typical psychotherapeutic services, rather than on adjunctive approaches to helping adult survivors.

CONCLUDING THOUGHTS

There are few conditions, in my judgment, troubling adults that require the kind of careful combination of human sensitivity and kindness with knowledge of facts that is needed in order to understand, assess, and treat the long-term effects of sexual abuse and exploitation in childhood by trusted persons.

We are a long way from reaching a state in which the younger and weaker are no longer abused by the older, larger, stronger, and more powerful. It is certainly no accident that the majority of abuse, sexual and physical, is perpetrated by males - adult males and younger males. Changes in attitudes that assign males a superior position are essential to significant alteration of abusive and exploitative patterns. No less than a drastic overhauling of cultural attitudes and values is required.

This is not to say that swift and effective intervention and punishment of perpetrators may not help, because there are some indications that it does in some instances and to some extent. It is to say that more basic and general changes that eradicate ideas of male dominance and replace them with equitable patterns of socialization for both genders are required in order to effect major change and provide opportunities for female and male children to grow up and develop their selfhood and sexuality appropriately and safely.

REFERENCES

Adams-Tucker, C., & Adams, P. L. (1984). Treatment of sexually abused children. In I. R. Stuart & J. G. Greer (Eds.), *Victims of Sexual Aggression* (pp. 57-64). New York: Van Nostrand Reinhold.

American Psychiatric Association. (1987). *Diagnostic and Statistical Manual of Mental Disorders* (3rd ed. rev.). Washington, DC: Author.

Banks, S. P., & Kahn, M. D. (1982). *The Sibling Bond.* New York: Basic Books.

Blume, S. (1990). *Secret Survivors: Uncovering Incest and Its Aftereffects in Women.* New York: John Wiley & Sons.

Bowen, M. (1978). *Family Therapy in Clinical Practice.* New York: Jason Aronson.

Briere, J. (1989). *Therapy for Adults Molested as Children: Beyond Survival.* New York: Springer.

Browne, A., & Finkelhor, D. (1986). The impact of child sexual abuse: A review of the research. *Psychological Bulletin, 99.*

Butler, S. (1986). *Conspiracy of Silence: The Trauma of Incest* (rev. ed.). Volcano, CA: Volcano Press.

Courtois, C. A. (1988). *Heal the Incest Wound: Adult Survivors in Therapy.* New York: Norton.

Crewdson, N. (1988). *By Silence Betrayed.* New York: Harper & Row.

Finkelhor, D. (1979). *Sexually Victimized Children.* New York: Free Press.

Finkelhor, D. (Ed.). (1984). *Child Sexual Abuse: New Theory and Research.* New York: Free Press.

Finkelhor, D. (1985). Sexual abuse and physical abuse: Some critical differences. In E. H. Newberger & R. Bourne (Eds.), *Unhappy Families* (pp. 21-30). Littleton, MA: PSG Publishing Co.

Finkelhor, D., & Browne, A. (1985). The traumatic impact of child sexual abuse: A conceptualization. *American Journal of Orthopsychiatry, 55,* 530-541.

Forward, S., & Buck, C. (1979). *Betrayal of Innocence: Incest and Its Devastation.* New York: Penguin.

Framo, J. L. (1982). *Explorations in Marital and Family Therapy: Selected Papers of James L. Framo.* New York: Springer.

Gelles, R. J. (1985). Family violence: What we know and can do. In E. H. Newberger & R. Bourne (Eds.), *Unhappy Families* (pp. 1-8). Littleton, MA: PSG Publishing Co.

Haggard, J. J., & Reppucci, K. D. (1988). *The Sexual Abuse of Children.* San Francisco: Jossey-Bass.

Hartman, C. R., & Burgess, A. W. (1986). Child sexual abuse: Generic rates of the victim experience. *Journal of Psychotherapy and the Family, 2,* 83-89.

Herman, J. (1981). *Father Daughter Incest.* Cambridge: Harvard University Press.

Kinsey, A. C., Pomeroy, W. B., Martin, C. E., & Gebhard, P. H. (1953). *Sexual Behavior in the Human Female.* Philadelphia: W. B. Saunders.

Lubianowicz, N. (1972). Paternal incest. *British Journal of Psychiatry, 120,* 301-313.

Madanes presents 15 steps for dealing with sex abuse. (1989, November/December). *Family Therapy News,* p. 19.

Nichols, W. C. (1988). *Marital Therapy: An Integrative Approach.* New York: Guilford.

Porter, R. (Ed.). (1984). *Child Sexual Abuse Within the Family.* London: Tavistock.

Russell, D. E. H. (1986). *The Secret Trauma: Incest in the Lives of Girls and Women.* New York: Basic Books.

Sgroi, S. M. (Ed.). (1982). *Handbook of Clinical Intervention in Sexual Abuse.* Lexington, MA: Lexington Books.

Silver, L. B., Dublin, C. C., & Lorrie, R. S. (1969). Does violence breed violence? *American Journal of Psychiatry, 126,* 404-407.

Tierney, K. J., & Corwin, D. L. (1983). Exploring intrafamilial child abuse. In D. Finkelhor, R. J. Gelles, G. T. Hotaling, &

M. A. Straus (Ed.), *The Dark Side of Families: Current Family Violence Research* (pp. 102-116). Beverly Hills, CA: Sage Publications.

Trepper, T. S., & Barrett, M. J. (1989). *Systematic Treatment of Incest: A Therapeutic Handbook.* New York: Brunner/Mazel.

Weinberg, S. K. (1976). *Incest Behavior* (rev. ed.). Secaucus, NJ: Citadel Press.

White, M. (1988/1989, Summer). The externalizing of the problem and the reauthoring of lives and relationships [Special issue]. *Dulwich Centre Newsletter.*

NOTES

NOTES

NOTES

NOTES

NOTES

Some Of The Other Titles Available From Professional Resource Press

Innovations in Clinical Practice: A Source Book - **11 Volumes**
    Hardbound edition (Vols. 3-11 only) per volume.. $54.20
    Looseleaf binder edition (Vols. 1-11) per volume... $59.20
Cognitive Therapy with Couples... $17.70
Maximizing Third-Party Reimbursement in Your Mental Health Practice................. $32.70
Who Speaks for the Children?
    The Handbook of Individual and Class Child Advocacy...................................... $38.70
Post-Traumatic Stress Disorder:
    Assessment, Differential Diagnosis, and Forensic Evaluation............................ $27.70
Clinical Evaluations of School-Aged Children: A Structured Approach to
    the Diagnosis of Child and Adolescent Mental Disorders.................................. $22.70
Stress Management Training: A Group Leader's Guide.. $14.70
Stress Management Workbook for Law Enforcement Officers.................................... $ 8.70
Fifty Ways to Avoid Malpractice:
    A Guidebook for Mental Health Professionals.. $17.70
Keeping Up the Good Work:
    A Practitioner's Guide to Mental Health Ethics... $16.70
Think Straight! Feel Great! 21 Guides to Emotional Self-Control............................. $14.70
Computer-Assisted Psychological Evaluations:
    How to Create Testing Programs in BASIC.. $22.70

Titles In Our Practitioner's Resource Series

Assessment and Treatment of Multiple Personality and Dissociative Disorders • Clinical Guidelines for Involuntary Outpatient Treatment • Cognitive Therapy for Personality Disorders: A Schema-Focused Approach • Dealing with Anger Problems: Rational-Emotive Therapeutic Interventions • Diagnosis and Treatment Selection for Anxiety Disorders • Neuropsychological Evaluation of Head Injury • Outpatient Treatment of Child Molesters • Pathological Gambling: Conceptual, Diagnostic, and Treatment Issues • Pre-Employment Screening for Psychopathology: A Guide to Professional Practice • *Tarasoff* and Beyond: Legal and Clinical Considerations in the Treatment of Life-Endangering Patients • Treating Adult Survivors of Childhood Sexual Abuse • What Every Therapist Should Know about AIDS
All books in this series are $11.70 each

All prices include shipping charges. Foreign orders add $2.00 shipping to total. All orders from individuals and private institutions must be prepaid in full. Florida residents add 7%. Prices and availability subject to change without notice.

See Reverse Side For Ordering Information ⟶

To Order

To order by mail, please send name, address, and telephone number, along with check or credit card information (card number and expiration date) to:

Professional Resource Press
PO Box 15560
Sarasota, FL 34277-1560

For fastest service
(VISA/MasterCard/American Express/Discover orders only)
CALL 1-813-366-7913 or FAX 1-813-366-7971

Would You Like To Be
On Our Mailing List?

If so, please write, call, or fax the following information:

Name: _____

Address: _____

Address: _____

City/State/Zip: _____

Daytime Phone #: (_____) _____

To insure that we send you all appropriate mailings, please include your professional affiliation (e.g., psychologist, clinical social worker, marriage and family therapist, mental health counselor, school psychologist, psychiatrist, etc.).